KU-110-960

"HOW TO CATCH THEM" SERIES

This is the most famous and best-selling series of books on angling ever published. They have been praised and recommended by *The Angling Times*, *The Field*, *Angling*, *Trout and Salmon*, *The Journal of the Flyfishers' Club*, *The Fishing Gazette*, *A.C.A. Quarterly Review*, *The Midland Angler*, *Angler's World*, *Gamekeeper and Countryside*, *The Fishing Tackle Dealer* and *Angler's Annual*.

The How To Catch Them books are edited by Kenneth Mansfield.

(continued overleaf)

TROUT
HOW TO CATCH THEM

By

W. A. ADAMSON

LONDON: HERBERT JENKINS

First published by
Herbert Jenkins Limited
2, Clement's Inn
London W.C.2
1955

Sixth Impression 1967

MADE AND PRINTED IN GREAT BRITAIN
BY D. R. HILLMAN & SONS LTD., FROME

CONTENTS

5

EDITOR'S FOREWORD

VERY few books indeed have been written about individual species of coarse fish, and the general aim of the " How to Catch Them " series is to fill this gap.

The statement is certainly untrue of trout, for more books have been written about these fish than any other single species throughout the world. There are scientific books on the structure, growth, feeding habits and breeding of trout: there are books on trout fishing with wet and dry fly, and exhaustive companion studies on natural flies and artificial fly tying: there are, too, scores of books of river lore, reminiscence and travel that have trout as their direct or unobtrusive backgrounds.

In view of this it may be wondered why a volume on trout has been included in the present series. There are good reasons. More and more people are turning to angling as a form of relaxation. More than ever before, coarse fish anglers are filling in the three months of their close season with trout fishing. Above all there is a growing realization that trout fishing is no longer a matter of long purses and exclusive waters, and that all who wish to do so may now fish for trout— and good trout—in a multitude of waters.

Ireland, Scotland and Wales abound in association, corporation, hotel and national trout fishing waters which can be fished by all-comers at a reasonable fee. In the north and west of

England similar facilities exist. Elsewhere in England it is difficult to get good river trout fishing, though several River Boards are taking action to remedy this defect. To a great extent it is counteracted by the numerous reservoirs that have been and are being constructed in all parts of the country, and whose fishing is open to all who are prepared to pay the necessary fee. This latter fact has produced a band of anglers who concentrate entirely upon fishing in lakes and reservoirs, and who have evolved a technique that differs in nearly all points from that of the river angler.

I know that many of the fishermen in these three groups are bewildered rather than helped by the wide choice of trout books open to them.

Mr. Adamson's book does not pretend to concentrate the wisdom of a thousand writers into a hundred pages. It gives a bird's eye view of the subject based on his own experience. It is simple, yet adequate. The angler who follows its precepts will be able to fish for trout with every hope of success. That, of course, is its essential aim, but the angler who desires also to delve into the wealth of trout angling literature available to him will, after reading this book, do so with an extremely useful framework of general trouting knowledge into which more advanced works will neatly fit.

K. M.

PREFACE

THE trout is one of the best known and most loved
of the angler's fishes. Described in 1496 as,
" a ryght deyntous fyssh and also a ryght fervente byter ", it has kept that reputation to the
present day. It is a vigorous, swift, lively, keen,
prolific, and robust fish, with a beautiful stream-
lined shape and a delicate colouring. It is also
one of the most widely distributed freshwater fish,
requiring only water that is reasonably cold and
clean, providing food for sustenance, and having
access to streams for breeding.

As soon as winter passes, trout are on the move
and begin to feed freely. Because of this, they
are vulnerable to a great variety of fishermen's
lures. As they are " ryght fervente byters," their
spirit of hearty co-operation in the sport of angling
has been rightly extolled in thousands of books.

At times, writers have credited trout with
remarkable powers of reasoning and organization.
That fashion has passed. The enthusiasm and
warm sentimentalizing have given place to a mood
of cold scientific inquiry. Like nearly everything
else, nowadays, the trout has been debunked.
He has survived this experience with a better
composure than many of his critics. Respect
still remains.

A grimly unsentimental friend of mine still
catches his first trout of the season with these
words, " Well done, stout trout! I return you
unharmed as a reward of valour." That sort of

thing is all very well. It is harmless nonsense and a trifle superstitious maybe. But it shows how trout affect human beings in strange ways. Unfortunately such faults as develop in this relationship of man and fish are all to be found on our side.

Some men have become snobs because of trout. Others have become butchers. Be warned. Folly of that kind is saddening, but it is set off by some generous impulses. Poets, artists, and philosophers have found inspiration in trout, and a great number of ordinary men have been led into paths of peace and quiet contemplation in pursuit of the graceful fish.

This is a small book. It is essentially practical and comprehensive. But it does not tell how to catch trout infallibly, at any time, and by all means. If it did, it would do the reader a great dis-service, for trout-fishing is an endless process of personal discoveries. Every honest book about fishing really tells the reader " how to find out how to catch fish." At the same time it should be made clear that this book is about trout, not in a vacuum or in Utopia, but in this present day and age.

The future, as always, is uncertain. Trout require clean, cold running water. In Britain water of any kind is becoming scarce. That seems almost unbelievable but it is true. Far more water is being needed and for a much greater variety of purposes than formerly. There are also more anglers than ever before, and they are using, not only the accumulated wisdom of past generations of anglers, but also the very latest products of human ingenuity in the way of

tackle. In years to come, will there be enough
trout-fishing for all of us? Can the trout survive?

The answers to these questions lie with the
readers of this book and with anglers in general.
This book tells how to catch trout. But merely
to put its precepts into practice will not make
anyone an angler. That title is reserved for those
who can read between the lines and understand
that the true angler must always fish with a sense
of respect to his craft, his fellows, and to the fish.
When trout can be caught too easily there is no
point in it. It is necessary to choose a difficult
fish and a difficult means of catching him. Personal skill can only be judged by a fastidious
interpretation of the legal phrase, "by fair
angling means". There is no credit and much
shame in destroying small, numerous, and easily-
caught trout nowadays.

On the other hand it is always a privilege to
participate in a sport created and protected by
great anglers of the past, and to try to ensure that
similar pleasure shall be available to anglers of
the future.

Let us be on our guard. Whenever anybody
tries to tell us nowadays that angling is " news ", or
politics, or business, or science, or an art, or a
problem, or a menace—turn a deaf ear. Angling
is none of these things. Angling is fun.

INTRODUCING THE TROUT

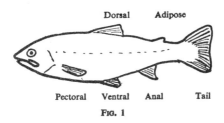

Dorsal　　Adipose

Pectoral　Ventral　Anal　　Tail

Fig. 1

THE BROWN TROUT

THERE are really only two kinds of trout, the brown trout and the sea-trout. The brown trout is confined to fresh water and the sea-trout spends much of its life in the sea. Under pressure of necessity, brown trout sometimes inhabit the brackish water of estuaries, and may even at times wander to the sea in search of food. This does not mean that a trout may become a sea-trout by accident or by " choice " so to speak. The descendants of brown trout remain brown trout, whereas sea-trout breed only sea-trout. The habit of running to the sea is hereditary. There is very little inter-breeding by the two kinds of trout, and the hybrid progeny are poor stock

13

and themselves often infertile. This book is not concerned with sea-trout.

It used to be thought that there were many different kinds of trout. Names were allotted to the trout of many localities in an attempt to distinguish between fish with superficial differences in appearance. Such superficial differences are due entirely to environment and feeding. It was shown repeatedly by experiment that trout, transferred from one place to another, very quickly lost their original appearance and acquired the characteristic "look" of the local inhabitants. As there was no basic differences in body structure or habit, naturalists very wisely decided to scrap all the fancy names, and to stick to the name, "brown trout" (*Salmo fario*) for all trout inhabiting fresh water. Anglers can avoid confusion and save trouble by following their example.

It sometimes happens that environment and feeding can produce an *apparent* difference in body structure, and then it may be found convenient to use a special name. The "gillaroo" trout, for example, is found in Scotland and Ireland. It is simply a brown trout whose diet consists to an unusual extent of small shell-bearing animals. This causes the development of a "gizzard" in the stomach-lining. Any normal trout can acquire this "gizzard" if put into a loch with the necessary high proportion of snails and molluscs in the feeding. Gillaroo trout lose this feature when removed from such waters. The process takes about two years.

The rainbow trout is a native of America. It has been imported in small numbers for introduction to some few British waters. It is a fine sporting fish. The main points of difference between the brown trout and the rainbow are that the latter eats more, grows more quickly, breeds later, and dies sooner than the brown trout. In structure there is little difference apart from the large liver occasioned by the heavier diet. In appearance the rainbow trout is notable for a purple iridescent sheen on its flanks and back.

RECOGNIZING THE TROUT

The brown trout is an extremely adaptable fish. That is to say, it is able to accommodate itself to many kinds of living conditions. This results in great variation of size and colour. A fully adult trout may be seven inches long and weigh but a few ounces or it may be forty inches long and

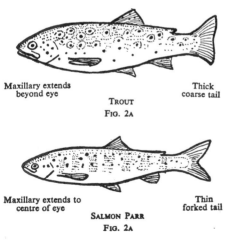

Maxillary extends
beyond eye

Thick
coarse tail

TROUT
FIG. 2A

Maxillary extends to
centre of eye

Thin
forked tail

SALMON PARR
FIG. 2A

weigh nearly thirty pounds. Some trout have black backs and greenish flanks. Others have light olive backs and golden sides with big black and red spots. Yet other specimens may have purplish backs and silvery flanks. Such variation is due to environment, which will be discussed later, because it is more important to learn how to distinguish a trout from its near relatives, the sea-trout and salmon.

This can easily be done by studying the diagrams in this chapter. They are designed to emphasize the points of difference. The first diagram shows the main features of the trout. This is followed

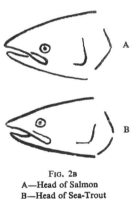

Fig. 2b
A—Head of Salmon
B—Head of Sea-Trout

by other diagrams in which details of these main features are shown in enlarged form for comparison with similar features of sea-trout and salmon.

BROWN TROUT

Has round black spots with pale ring, and often has red spots too.

Anal fin has white border on forward edge.

Has a pinkish tip to the adipose fin.

Has comparatively large head.

Has white or pink flesh.

SEA TROUT

Has X-shaped black spots without pale ring.

Anal fin without white border.

Has a yellowish tip to the adipose fin.

Has comparatively small head.

Has reddish or orange flesh.

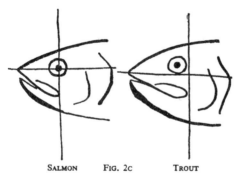

SALMON   FIG. 2c   TROUT

The *typical* brown trout has an olive-green back with bronze and gold sides. The *typical* sea-trout is bluish-green merging into a bright silver on the flanks.

B

Here is the "acid-test" for deciding whether
a fish is a trout or a salmon. It is necessary to
count the number of scales between the adipose
fin and the lateral line.

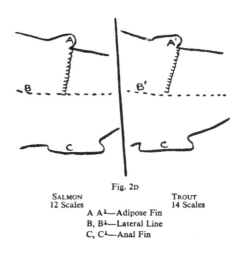

Fig. 2D

SALMON	TROUT
12 Scales	14 Scales

A A¹—Adipose Fin
B, B¹—Lateral Line
C, C¹—Anal Fin

Salmon (*Salmo salar*) will have ten to thirteen
scales (usually eleven or twelve).
Brown Trout (*Salmo fario*) and Sea-Trout
(*Salmo trutta*) will have thirteen to sixteen
scales (usually fourteen).

The centre of a salmon's eye is on a level with
the tip of its snout. In addition, when the mouth
is closed, the maxillary bone (visible on the outside
of the upper jaw) extends beyond the eye in the
trout, but not in the salmon. These two features
give the salmon the appearance of having a small
head and mouth.

In the salmon, the " wrist " of the tail and the tail itself appear to be finer and more slender than in the trout. The trout's tail is coarser and is not slightly " forked " as it is in the case of the salmon.

These points may seem hard to follow from verbal description, but they are quite obvious on the fish and in diagrams.

PROTECTIVE COLOUR

The delicate colouring of trout is caused by the action of light working through the eye of the fish and affecting a substance called guanin in its skin. This process enables the fish to achieve a high degree of protective colouration. The back of the fish is dark and the belly is almost white. The effect of this is to approximate the shade of the fish to the prevailing tint of its background, and thus make it hard to see. Quite often the presence of a trout is betrayed only by the flash of the white belly seen as the fish turns quickly when making a dash for " cover ".

DISTRIBUTION OF TROUT

The brown trout is found throughout the temperate zone of the northern hemisphere. It has been successfully introduced to parts of the southern hemisphere (notably New Zealand) and even to high-altitude regions of the tropics.

Trout inhabit the pebbly brooks of the moors and fells. They are equally at home in the slow-moving weedy waters of deep broad rivers. They are to be found in the wide loughs of Ireland

and in the deep narrow lochs of the Scottish Highlands. In the dirty brick-lined courses of rivers passing through big cities, they have been known to thrive and to attain great weight. In man-made reservoirs, in estuaries, in ponds, mill-leads and ditches, trout have been found. They seem to be able to tolerate a slowly increasing pollution of their stream, but sudden transition from comparative purity to gross pollution will usually prove fatal.

Being strong and well shaped for the purpose, trout are able to withstand strong currents and spates. They are active and mobile fish, revelling in water moved by wind and current. They cannot live in stagnant pools lined with weeds and decaying vegetation, because they need plenty of oxygen. In order to breed they must have access to fine gravel permeated by clear running water.

THE " TOUGHNESS " OF TROUT

From the foregoing it will be understood that the trout is both adaptable and robust. An impression is sometimes given of the trout as a delicate creature, an easy prey for its many enemies, and prone to all manner of weakness and disease. This is quite wrong. The trout is well able to look after itself given a reasonable chance to do so. It can survive extreme cold, semi-starvation, rough handling, injury and disease. It can also withstand considerable shock and sudden tremendous increases in pressure.

Barren lakes in Canada have been successfully

stocked with young trout dropped into them from aeroplanes at some height above the water. Experiments have recently been made showing that trout can pass through parts of hydro-electric plants without damage.

Although the trout " can take it ", there is a time-honoured and wholly admirable convention among anglers which demands that trout should at all times be handled with care. Fishermen are punctilious in trying to ensure that everything possible should be done to encourage the survival of adequate breeding stocks. It is the custom for anglers to wet their hands before removing immature trout from the hook, and to return them gently to the water. Dry hands and rough handling might conceivably damage the fish and render them vulnerable to disease. No sensible person connives at or tolerates the pollution of trout waters or such short-sighted stupidities as the poaching, poisoning, or netting of fish.

The impression that trout are delicate creatures appears to have arisen as the result of man's experience in the rearing of trout artificially in hatcheries. In the early days these hatchery-trout, like the sons of some rich men, had a great deal done for them, and were protected from the harsh realities of life. When they were turned loose it was found that they had failed to develop any resistance to hardship and disease. They had not learned to fend for themselves, and were unable to compete for food with other fish. They could not recognize their natural enemies, and were guileless victims of deception, subject to all kinds of unpleasant surprises many of which proved fatal. In short, fish of that kind might be said to have started life with every possible disadvantage.

An amusing story comes from America this year. An angling club had its water stocked with hatchery-bred trout. When anglers began to stalk cautiously along the banks of the stream with their rods, they were amazed to find the fish rushing towards them in shoals. The fish saw the men and, quite understandably, they came near the bank expecting to be fed as they had been in the hatchery ponds. They could be caught by the crudest methods with the anglers moving about in full view and at short range. With typical American ingenuity a scheme was devised whereby the fish were made artificially " wild " by being given electric shocks instead of the food they had learned to expect.

There is a moral to all this. The best modern hatchery practice tends to reproduce natural conditions so far as possible. Anglers now know that the first consideration in preserving angling water is the expansion and protection of its natural facilities for breeding trout in the wild state. There is, of course, an enormous wastage in natural breeding, and it is seldom necessary or even possible to make good this wastage by planting hatchery-bred fish. Moreover, trout which have been brought up the hard way are at once better breeding-stock and more sporting quarry from the angler's point of view.

CHAPTER II

SPAWNING, GROWTH AND FEEDING

SPAWNING

IN Britain the brown trout's breeding period varies from October to February. Its onset is determined by the physical condition of the fish, and that is influenced by climatic conditions affecting the food supply. As winter comes on and temperatures fall, trout begin to gather in shoals. The instinct to " run " to small, shallow, gravelly streams seems to be prompted by the influx of appreciably colder water flowing from higher ground.

Female fish reach the redds in advance of the males and select sites on gravel on which the largest pebbles may be about three inches in diameter with much finer material in the spaces between pebbles. When they are joined by single males coming alongside them, the females cause shallow depressions to be made in the gravel, and deposit their eggs, which are then fertilized by the male. It is noteworthy that the fish select and use only sites in which the gravel is permeated by a continuous flow of water.

The young trout hatch from the egg in from one to three month's time according to the temperature of the water. They are known as alevins at this stage and have a yolk-sac attached to their bodies. This gradually disappears as the small fish begin to feed on microscopic organisms in the water.

After spawning the spent fish drop down slowly to the still deeps of rivers and lakes. They are weak and in poor condition until March when food becomes more plentiful.

GROWTH AND FEEDING

Nothing brings trout into good condition more quickly than a diet of " flies ". This is most important from the angler's point of view. It will be necessary to discuss what these " flies " are, and when they appear, later, but because trout eat a great many other things besides flies, it should be realized that their fly-diet plays a very special part in their regaining condition after spawning. Why this should be so, is not quite clear, but a surprising parallel is to be found in the case of pike. Shortly after spawning, pike have been found to be literally crammed with a mass of minute freshwater shrimps, so that it would seem as though food of a larger and heavier kind is avoided by some fish after the " fast " which takes place at spawning-time.

Very young trout feed on animal and vegetable plankton. Plankton is a name used to cover great numbers of microscopic forms of life which are produced in water. Plankton is absorbed through the mouth and " filtered " from the water by " rakers " on the gills of the fish. As trout continue to grow they feed on progressively larger creatures, but even mature trout retain their fly-eating propensity until they are well on in years.

The whole question of growth and size of trout is dependent on feeding and water-temperature. Trout become torpid in water that is either very cold or very warm. They grow biggest and most quickly in places where there is an equable water temperature (say, between 50 and 65 degrees Fahrenheit) throughout the greater part of the year, combined with abundance of feeding in considerable variety. In artificial conditions it is possible to rear a trout weighing two pounds in two years. On the other hand, trout from peaty tarns at high altitude may weigh less than half a pound when seven years old. Seven-year-old trout weighing twenty pounds have been caught in deep lakes.

Shallow water near sea-level, with good feeding will produce fish of approximately one pound in from four to five years, and trout of this kind form the great majority of those caught by anglers in Britain. Where there are too many trout for the food which is available, the average size of the fish will remain small. This can often be increased by reducing the number of fish.

Trout have been known to live for fifteen years. In Loch Leven fish older than seven years tend to " go back " in condition, and there are not many trout surviving beyond that age.

The process of angling very largely consists in deceiving a fish by presenting to it something which it will mistake for food. For this reason it is important to know what trout feed on. Here is a list: plankton, the larvæ of insects, flies, moths, beetles, caterpillars, grasshoppers, minnows, sticklebacks, crayfish, shrimps, snails, leeches, fish ova, elvers, perch-fry, tadpoles, frogs,

matchsticks, coal, bacon and onions. This is not
a leg-pull. The last four items were only a *few*
of the strange things taken from the stomach of a
three-pound trout. I have included them at the
end of the list to show that trout are not so fussy
as they are sometimes represented to be. Fish
have small brains designed chiefly to respond
quickly to external stimuli, and when they eat
things like coal and matchsticks no doubt they
do so just because such objects have come to
them in the water in the way that a good deal of
other food comes to them.

This does not mean that coal and onions are
to be recommended as baits. The great majority
of trout will never encounter such things in a
lifetime, but they *will* meet flies and insect-larvæ
in very large numbers, and they *may* feel inclined
to investigate anything which comes to them in a
naturally water-borne manner.

From April onwards mature trout move
actively in search of food and quickly regain
condition. During this time they will find much
of their food on the bottom, some in mid-water,
and some on the surface. Quite often they travel
miles from their usual haunts in response to
changes in water level and in exploring potential
sources of food. They reach a peak of condition about mid-summer, but continue to feed
right on to late autumn when low temperatures
and the spawning instinct reassert a depressive
influence.

Fishermen often refer to big trout, particularly
if they are lank and lean with big heads, as
" cannibal-trout ". This is quite misleading.
The fact is that *all* trout are cannibals or potential

cannibals. Trout which have grown up together do not usually attack each other, but any trout of almost any size will attack and try to eat other trout, particularly in times of food scarcity. It is a commonplace to find trout a few inches long which have choked in the attempt to swallow trout only a trifle smaller than themselves. The long, thin, dark-coloured trout with " underslung " jaw and disproportionately large head, is simply a trout which has been " going back " in condition for some time. It has been unable to find food easily and in sufficient quantities to maintain its weight.

The enormous trout which appear in all lists of " notable trout " come mainly from the deep lochs of Scotland and Ireland. Malloch of Perth, who handled a great many fish of this type, stated that he had never found them to contain anything but one or two small fish, presumably small trout or char. Nevertheless trout of this kind are caught in Ireland by " dapping " the may-fly or daddy-long-legs, and similar trout are occasionally caught on fly in Scotland in the autumn. This type of trout (sometimes called " ferox ") inhabits deep lakes and appears to subsist mainly on smaller fish, although the habit of rising to surface food may not be entirely lost.

Apart from these trout of the deep lakes weighing from six to thirty pounds or more, there are trout of from four to ten pounds caught every year in rivers, lakes and reservoirs all over the country. Such catches are usually reported in the Press and the fish are exceptional. They must be regarded as the hardy few survivors of their own generation, and no doubt they owe a great deal to luck, good feeding, and a tough constitution.

In order to practice their deceptions, anglers must study the food habits of trout. They do not attempt the impossible task of presenting imitations of plankton, but they do successfully contrive imitations of insect-larvæ, flies, and small fish.

Although much is known about the feeding habits of trout, there are still plenty of obscurities and mysteries to intrigue the angler. Great heat or cold inhibits feeding. Trout are not inclined to feed on the surface in bright sunlight, before a thunderstorm, or when the barometer is falling. A rising glass, cloudy sky and steady breeze are thought to be good signs, and yet the fact remains that trout have been caught at times in all kinds of weather and even throughout rapidly changing conditions.

At dawn and dusk trout seem especially disposed to feed on the surface, but it is not clear whether this propensity is due to conditions of light, temperature, pressure, or changes in the oxygen-content of the water. The greatest concentration of plankton in lakes occurs in a " layer " of water the position of which seems to vary throughout the day. This begs the question, do fish invariably feed when food is available? The answer is, that they do not.

Fish of the salmonidæ species (to which trout belong) appear to fast in freshwater during the winter and to some extent while breeding, but it is not certain whether or not they may continue to maintain condition by a reduced diet involving plankton-feeding. There is also the question of osmosis. A goldfish will live longer in water in which other fish have lived as compared with sterile water or water in which fish have not previously lived. The word " osmosis " means the interchange of place of two fluids separated by a permeable partition, each tending to pass through the latter at a rate determined by their respective densities. The skin of a trout is a " permeable " partition, and while fish can feed avidly and gain weight quickly when plenty of food is available, it seems also to be obvious that they can endure a condition of starvation which would be quickly fatal to warm-blooded land animals. This is borne out by the common example of the aged fingerlings often found in mountain tarns.

These matters may seem to be far removed from considerations of practical angling. The fact is that nothing concerning the feeding habits of trout is beyond the angler's interest and this brief mention of such obscurities is made to show that the study of fish is anything but simple. It is always worth while examining the " crop " of a trout to find out on what it has been feeding. In that way a logical decision can be made regarding lures and methods of fishing, and it is with methods that we are now concerned.

CHAPTER III

METHODS OF CATCHING TROUT

ILLEGAL WAYS AND IMMORAL WILES

THE words " fair angling means " exclude the use
of nets, spears, traps, lights, trimmers, otter-
boards, cross-lines, electrical devices, lime,
poisons, and the use of any fish-roe as bait.
That list is by no means complete. All of these
methods have been, very rightly, prohibited by
law, because they have all been used at some time
or other in order to catch fish easily and cheaply.
Angling is not a means of catching fish easily or
cheaply, and whereas there is very little public or
free fishing in England, Wales or Ireland, there
is absolutely *no* free fishing whatsoever in Scotland,
except in the sea.

That is the law although very few people seem
to know it. It is good law too, for in these over-
crowded islands, all wild animals, birds, and fish
must be regarded as living on " sufferance ".
That is to say, they are " protected ", because if
they were not protected all of them possessing
any value as food or otherwise would be very
quickly exterminated. Such a loss would be
tragic indeed, and so everybody owning and
maintaining property on which wild creatures are
able to breed, is deserving of public respect and
legal support.

It is, of course, much cheaper to buy trout than
to angle for them, and this fact also, is not nearly

so widely known as it might be. I have met many people who think that angling is a way of obtaining " something for nothing ", and even more people who strongly resent paying a reasonable sum for their fishing. Many of them gladly disgorge exorbitant fees for entertainment of less value. It seems to be an old British custom which is dying hard and tardily.

The right way to catch trout is to catch them legally and pay gladly for the privilege of doing so. But it is not enough merely to keep to the rules. As in every other game and sport, one must also observe the etiquette. As most fishings are private, the " form " may be printed on the ticket in the shape of bye-laws, but where that is not done, it must be left to the good sense of the angler to see that everything is done decently and in good order.

The trout is a bold and inquisitive fish, but he would be an absolute " sucker " for handfuls of ground-bait followed by the offer of maggots on fine tackle! That would be too easy. How long it would last and how roach-tackle would stand up to a two-pound trout is another matter, but bottom-fishing, ground-bait, floats, ledgers and paternosters are not permissible in trout-fishing.

That is not to say that bait-fishing for trout is taboo. Worms, creepers, grasshoppers and grubs can be legitimately used for trout, but only in special circumstances. Take worms, for example. When a stream is in heavy spate the water rises quickly and for the first few hours it may be of a thick opaque mud-colour. There are rivers where these conditions at once attract a crowd of pseudo-anglers to the river bank. They sit right

on the water side and dangle worms in the turbid
stream with the crudest of tackle. In such conditions it would be possible to use hand-lines.
They catch trout, but there is no sport, skill or
merit in the act. The colour of the water prevents the fish seeing the operator (he cannot be
called an angler) and disguises the crudities of
tackle, while the noise of a stream in spate makes
caution superfluous and the strength of the
current and opacity of the water renders control
of the bait impossible. The whole process is
like a dip in a lucky-bag. Apart from being in
the fresh air, no benefit can accrue to those who
dangle worms in deep coloured water. If they
value their time and want fish they would find it
cheaper to buy them.

In despising spate-fishers-for-trout, I make one
exception. Small boys under twelve years old
are entitled to some indulgence. All their
activities which involve risk and enterprise should
not be too severely discouraged provided they
are not positively anti-social and diabolic.
Let them be chidden and directed, but do not curb
a natural curiosity and desire for experiment.
The under-twelve who dangles a worm in coloured
water, is, like any dog, entitled to one bite.

As things are at present, it is bad practice to
catch a great many trout at any one time. It is
wrong to spoil the water for other anglers by
using maggots or by slaughtering undersized
trout by spinning a lure from a fixed-spool reel.
Many angling associations have been compelled
to make strict rules banning such undesirable
activities, but the obligation to fish fairly rests
primarily with the individual angler.

FAIR ANGLING MEANS

Rod and line can be used in a great variety of ways to catch trout. There are three broad divisions, bait-fishing, fly fishing, and spinning. In every case the object is to present to a trout in its natural haunt, something which it will mistake for food present in the water without artificial aid, but which is in fact something concealing a hook attached to a line in the angler's control.

BAIT FISHING: WORMS

Worms are good bait in any month of the season, but they are usually used in July and August when low water and warm weather make trout disinclined to rise to fly. There are many kinds of worms. Fresh lively pinkish worms about two inches long are the best, and they should be mounted on either a Stewart or Pennel Tackle in preference to a single hook. (Fig. 3.)

Using a longish rod, short line and a yard of nylon cast, the angler fishes upstream in clear shallow water. Moving slowly and keeping out of sight of the fish, he swings rather than casts the bait ahead of him, aiming to cause the worm to be borne downstream towards him as if by the current. The line should not be tight and the bait should not be " worked ", but the worm must come downstream ahead of the cast and line, and on or close to the bottom.

This is difficult. The angler must be cautious in order not to alarm the fish, yet he must be able to aim the worm by a slow swing (so that it does not flick off the hook) into suitable places such as under the lee of rocks and boulders, the edge of

c

STEWART TACKLE   PENNEL TACKLE

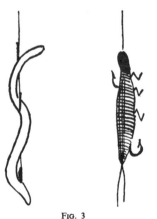

FIG. 3

WORM ON
STEWART TACKLE

CREEPER ON
PENNEL TACKLE

eddies, the tail of pools and runs, and other obvious lies. Whenever the line checks, pause and then tighten quickly. The whole business calls for stalking, precision and concentration.

GRUBS, CATERPILLARS, GRASSHOPPERS, etc.

These can be used in the same way as worms, but it will be found that the utmost care must be taken to keep such fragile baits on the hook for even a few " casts " at a time. Baits of this kind are more suitable for tackling rivers which are lined with thick bushes, trees, and heavy undergrowth.

On a still warm day it will be possible to use a short rod and find small openings between the bushes where the rod can be inserted over deep water and the bait " dibbed " on the surface or allowed to sink slowly. A short fine cast and small single hook will suffice. One or two split shot can be nipped on the cast if it is desired to make the bait sink. The larvæ of the stone-fly (called creepers) can be used in this way mounted on a Pennel Tackle.

Big trout can be taken on a dead minnow fished on the " sink-and-draw " plan. It should be mounted on a small leaded " flight " with a tiny treble hook at the tail and another hooked into the body of the minnow. The bait is allowed to fall slowly to the bottom and is then drawn to the surface in a series of jerks.

Used legitimately all of these methods will take trout, but they are not infallible, nor are they suited to every kind of water for every day of the season. Fine tackle is needed and the kind of common-sense fieldcraft which outdoor people find pleasure in exercising.

PRESENTATION AND DISCRETION IN BAIT FISHING

As the angler's object is to " present " his counterfeit food to the trout in a natural way—as if it were food coming to the fish in a manner which experience has taught the fish to expect—it will be obvious that the angler must use rod and tackle of a kind most likely to help him in achieving that object. So far, I have mentioned rods and lines as being short or long, but a more detailed description is given later in this book when it deals with rods and tackle. A very good presentation of the baits so far mentioned can also be made by methods which come under the heading of " spinning ". These also will be fully explained later. They are mentioned now because I want to emphasize a point which is very seldom made clear to the beginner in trout-fishing.

Angling is a pleasure. Therefore the angler should use methods which give him enjoyment. These will not always be methods likely to produce most fish, but as the pleasure in a mere acquisition of dead fish is not really so important as the exercise of skill, the angler will do well to try everything at least once, and then concentrate to some extent on the things he likes doing best.

Some people like making their own tackle and enjoy manipulating rather complicated devices involving tackle of extreme delicacy and fineness perhaps, but which may involve dependence to a greater or lesser extent on mechanism. Some people dislike handling worms and insects and impaling them on hooks. It is well known that people differ greatly in temperament, and whereas some enjoy mastering complexities, others prefer to use simple methods which leave them unencumbered and more free to develop a purely physical skill in the use of equipment. The beginner should inquire into the methods of other anglers, investigate and try them for himself, and then use his own discretion in doing what he likes to do best.

Quite recently a very skilful and well-known angler became convinced that certain methods (which he had done much to perfect himself) would quickly oust all other methods from popular favour. As things turned out, that did not happen. A great many people simply could not be bothered with the elaborate contrivances in which he took such delight. They greatly preferred a simplicity which gave them more pleasure. In the long history of trout-fishing it has been shown time after time that there need be no compulsion by fashion or advertising. People do what they like to do. One man's meat is another man's poison.

FLY FISHING: GENERAL

Worms, grubs, snails, and small fish are common trout-foods. Some of them live in the water and others fall into it. This is also true of a great number of insects which anglers call " flies " for convenience. Trout eat the many varieties of house-fly when they get the chance, but there are literally hundreds of thousands of kinds of flies which trout would also eat, and a great many which they habitually encounter.

It is worth remembering that more than two thousand years ago men wrote about trout rising to flies, and also told how it was possible to catch trout by concealing a small hook in an imitation fly and casting it upon the water. This has been brought almost to a fine art in Britain, and some of the flies described in the earliest English books hundreds of years ago, can be recognized as the prototypes of flies which anglers use to-day.

There are, in particular, five kinds of flies which especially interest the angler, because they lay their eggs in or near the water, and for that reason are met with by trout at an early age, and are eaten more or less avidly throughout their lifetime. Four of these groups of flies lay their eggs actually in the water, and trout eat not only the eggs, but the larvæ and the growing fly at all stages of its development. Some of these eggs are laid on reeds and water-weeds, others are laid on the bottom, where they hatch out into tiny grubs or creepers. Some go through a chrysalis stage, and all eventually come to the surface of the water again, where they use wings as mature flies in order to mate and continue the cycle.

Examples of these five groups of flies are shown together along with a table explaining differences in their structure. The names of the groups are, *Ephemeridæ*, *Trichoptera*, *Sialidæ*, *Perlidæ*, and *Diptera*. The names do not matter much. It is more important to be able to recognize the flies as trout-food, and to be able to tell flies in one group from those in another.

When the time comes for a " setting " of fly-eggs
in a river bed to reach (through several slow
stages) a stage of maturity, the insects, all within
a matter of an hour or two, struggle up through
the water to the surface.   There they lie, shedding
their sheaths while light and air strengthen their
wings and they take off in flight for the mating-
dance.   That is to say, what is known as a
" hatch of fly " occurs.   The water is full of
thousands of insects in all stages of approach to
the surface and take-off.   This process takes
place, day after day throughout spring, summer
and autumn, according to the time when eggs have
been laid and according to the season favoured
by members of the various groups of insects.

Trout feed on these creatures avidly, and
obviously they must consume enormous quantities of them.   Therein lies the angler's opportunity.   If he can imitate a fly of this kind suffici-
ently well to deceive a trout into thinking that it
is one of the crowd, he stands a fair chance of
catching it.   The angler may choose to " present "
his imitation fly at any stage of its progress from
the bottom to the surface and thereafter.   It
should be noted that even in this short journey
the creatures undergo striking changes in
appearance.

Throughout the ages and to this day, anglers
have devoted great care in studying the habits
and appearance of these flies, and they have
shown unending patience and ingenuity in making
imitations.   Viewed under the microscope alongside the genuine article, even the best of these
imitations is not really very like the original, but
most of them are near enough for all practical

purposes. Trout *are* fussy, but they cannot afford to be *too* fussy. They must eat, and when food is available they make the most of their time in a competitive market, sucking in fly after fly as fast as they can before their neighbours take them, and before the " hatch " comes to an end.

Although a " rise " to a " hatch " of fly is the angler's opportunity, there are certain disadvantages. If flies coming through the water are nearly all of one type, the trout will be looking for that type only and may ignore an imitation of another group. If the hatch is at its height and the water is literally covered with flies, the angler's imitation may be only one among many and will stand a poor chance of being selected. Of course trout will often take a single fly although no hatch is taking place, and trout will often concentrate on taking the insects *on their way to the top* while ignoring them when they arrive there—and vice versa.

Fly fishing is not really difficult (comparatively speaking) and it is even possible to " fluke " an occasional trout without troubling to study the situation, but one of the main fascinations in fly fishing is the opportunity it gives for acute observation of what is going on and acting appropriately.

The fly fisher then, must present an imitation of a fly which trout are expecting to see, or which they may be presumed to be expecting, and he must present it at the time and in the places and in the guise and in the manner favoured by the natural insect. The more he knows about the natural insect and its habits, the better. First-hand knowledge is best, for although there are scores of good books on the subject, flies and their habits change according to district and season, and the angler cannot really understand what he is trying to do unless he has caught and examined the actual flies from the water where he hopes to catch trout.

In recent years bird-watching has assumed the proportions of a " craze " in this country. Trout-and-fly watching is the fisherman's equivalent. There is no need to overdo things or to take copious notes. By remaining still and by keeping quiet, it is possible to find out what kind of trout are in the water, where they are lying and what they are feeding on.

Fly fishing is a most attractive way of catching trout. In recent years many beginners have concentrated on bait-fishing and on spinning as being easier and more productive. The same thing has happened with salmon fishing, but the truth of the matter is probably this. If people took the trouble to overcome the essential problem—presenting an attractive lure at the right depth—fly fishing could be made just as productive as other methods. It is worth while noting that there is no real basis for supposing that spinning is more productive.

THE WET FLY

This name is used to distinguish the technique from dry fly fishing. In dry fly fishing it is usual to oil the fly to keep it on the surface of the water and to prevent it sinking. As a general rule one fly is used and the line is greased, and all but the last six inches of the " leader ", for the same

reason. In wet fly fishing, the fly may be fished
on the surface or at any depth all the way down
to the bottom. The line is not greased for
floating, and two, three, or even four flies may be
used.

The object of wet fly fishing is to present one or
more artificial flies to a trout so that it accepts one
as a natural insect. The method can be used on

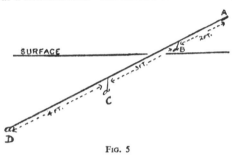

FIG. 5

A—Junction of leader and reel line.
B—Bob Fly.
C—Dropper.
D—Tail Fly.

brooks, rivers, lakes, estuaries, and reservoirs.
A rod of from ten to twelve feet long is most
suitable and most people prefer one in which the
" action " (i.e. the degree and distribution of
suppleness) can be felt right down to the butt.
The line should be of dressed silk or dressed
nylon and should be of a weight to match the rod.
These matters will be dealt with more fully later.
A cast or leader of gut or nylon is attached to the
end of the line and one fly is attached, to the end
of this, and one or two others by means of short
lengths of gut at intervals. (Fig. 5).

Provided the wind is favourable (and sometimes when it is not) it is best to fish upstream on streams and rivers. The angler who first wrote about the advantages of fishing upstream was a Scot named Stewart. When a friend of his asked his keeper what it was like to go for a day's fishing with Mr. Stewart, the man replied, " It is twelve hours of creeping and crawling! "

These words contain the first essential of fly fishing. It is possible to stand stock still within a few feet of trout without alarming them, but the trouble arises in getting there! It is no good being shy or afraid of looking foolish. Crawl if necessary. Keep out of sight and move slowly with the utmost caution. Try to keep the light in your face and avoid casting shadows on the water, or making the bank vibrate with a heavy tread.

Trout lie in water facing the direction from which water is flowing. There are usually currents even in lakes and still water. Near the surface, wind may cause a current and trout will face the wind, but two or three feet below, there may be a different current. In still water trout face away from the source of light; near the surface they cruise against the wind in search of food: at deeper levels, they swim in any direction but usually head away from the source of light.

The object of a wet fly fisher is to present imitation flies in the water at depths and in ways and in places in which trout may be expecting to find natural insects. He does this by casting in front of him and manipulating rod and line so that his flies appear in the water as trout expect to find them.

THE DRY FLY

The dry fly fisher seeks only to present an imitation of a fly on the *surface* of the water, that is, an imitation of an insect which has alighted on the water, or has come through it from below and is floating on the top. His fly is *dry* but it is, in fact, usually oiled or treated in some way to prevent it sinking. In ideal conditions, he observes a trout rising to eat flies floating on the top, and uses an imitation of the type of fly on which it is feeding. He then casts this imitation so that it alights on the water and floats down directly over the trout, which then takes his imitation fly and is hooked. If he sees a trout which is not rising, or if he cannot see a trout at all, he may cast his imitation in such places as may contain trout in hope that one will rise and be hooked.

NYMPH FISHING

Nymphs are flies coming to the surface of the water, but which have not unsheathed their wings. There is no great difference between nymph fishing and wet fly fishing, except that the strict nymph fisher uses what he hopes is a near imitation of the actual insect on which he observes trout to be feeding. He also will aim at a feeding trout and will use usually one nymph on his cast.

DAPPING

In dapping for trout the fisherman uses a long light rod, but does not " cast " a heavy line with it. The line is of floss silk or cotton and this is blown by the wind out in front of the angler. To the end of this blow-line is attached a short length of gut or nylon with the fly and hook at the end of it. Merely by a gentle inclination of his long rod, the angler allows his fly to alight on the water. He may cause it to skip and move from place to place in the same way. The fly may be either a natural insect (may-fly or daddy-long-legs) or it may be an artificial fly.

SPINNING

In spinning the angler casts a bait into the water and causes it to move through the water towards him by pulling the line in—usually by winding it in on to a reel. The bait may be a worm or a minnow or one of a great many arti-ficial lures intended to represent a trout-food. In order to disguise the hooks on such baits, " fins " are sometimes fitted which cause the bait to spin rapidly, hence the term " spinning ". Nowadays baits are used which do not spin, but the general name is still used.

The rods, reels and lines used for fly fishing are not suitable for spinning, and nowadays this form of angling has its own very specialized equipment.

CHAPTER IV

FLIES

GENERAL

THERE are at least five good reasons for trout eating flies. They are, hunger, aggressiveness, curiosity, jealousy and habit. Hunger is easily understood. Aggressiveness is a natural animal instinct, whereby the intrusion of any smaller, weaker form of life into a trout's " territory " is resented, and the intruder is attacked. Curiosity plays a part. Fish bite something which appears to be good to eat in order to find out if they are right. If they are wrong, they promptly eject it. Jealousy arises in the presence of other fish. Experiments have often been made with a well-fed trout in a tank. If the fish is absolutely replete with food and food is put in the tank, the trout will ignore it. If another *trout* is then put in the tank, the well-fed trout will immediately take the food before the new arrival can do so. As so much of a fish's time is taken up in a search for food, its reaction to the sight of potential food is almost automatic. Food, after all, is its main interest in life.

Trout have small and primitive brains. They are great eaters but poor thinkers. They are *not* expert entomologists with an enthusiastic appreciation of the niceties of artificial fly-making and it is ridiculous to pretend that they are. A trout which has " refused " three patterns of a fly and accepts a third one, has most likely been deterred by sight of the leader or line. Trout become " educated " or wary simply as a natural reaction from an unpleasant experience, not as a result of thought and introspection.

For more than fifty years dry fly fishermen have taken a great deal of pleasure in striving to offer trout exact imitations of the flies on which they are feeding at any given time. These anglers have made a great contribution to angling, but much of their work is discredited to-day. A man spending equal amounts of time fishing wet fly and dry fly, will take up to three times more fish on wet fly. Obsession with exact imitation is a waste of time. Wet fly fishing is the more difficult branch and it involves a greater variety of techniques. Dry fly fishing is a simple process and very attractive to practise. It has greatly suffered from the obscurantism of its most enthusiastic adherents.

The story is told how one well-known dry fly angler turned renegade. He fished throughout a whole season with a fly known as Red Quill. He did quite well. I feel sure that anybody who chose to use nothing but a Greenwell's Glory in three sizes, wet or dry, would not go far wrong.

A SHORT PRACTICAL COURSE IN TROUT FLIES

What is the best and quickest way nowadays for a beginning angler to learn something about trout flies? Must he study the whole natural history rigmarole of the ephemeridea, trichoptera, perlidæ and diptera? I think not. He should examine flies on the water he proposes to fish. He should study the creatures he will find under flat stones at the bottom, and he should observe the kind of insects to be found on trees and grasses by the waterside. That should give him some idea of the size and type of insect he is anxious to imitate.

Let him also pay a visit to the shop of a fishing-tackle dealer. He should do this, not with the object of buying a lot of flies, nor even to ask the dealer how many he ought to have, but simply in order to see some artificial flies and to get some advice.

It will be a poor dealer indeed who cannot produce a catalogue containing coloured plates of flies, and it will be a very short-sighted dealer who makes any charge for supplying one. The dealer's livelihood depends on satisfying anglers' wants and attending to their inquiries. There may be some doubt about the best baits for fish, but there is no doubt that one of the finest baits for anglers is a really good fishing-tackle catalogue!

Winged flies, hackle flies, wet and dry flies, stream, river and lake flies may all be depicted with their differences and variations. If the inquirer can see a few of the actual flies and hear what the dealer has to say about local conditions, he should learn a lot.

Trout flies are pretty things and there are hundreds of patterns. Some of the simplest are the most effective. A very few strands of black feather tied to a small hook is called a Black Spider. It will catch trout large and small from brook, river and lake. It does not look like a spider and it is not intended to represent one.

The explanation is that in water it looks like a " nymph " which is a name for insects on their way from the bottom to the surface of the water. Reddish or mottled feather is used to dress similar spiders which are also proven killers.

A study of a good catalogue showing the flies with their names, and an examination of any dealer's stock, shows how anglers contrive to imulate flies which trout feed on. Three things should be clear at once. All sorts of materials such as feather, silk, quill, cellulite, hair, fur, wool, wire, tinsel, plastics, and nylon fibre have been pressed into use. Secondly, flies of all shapes and sizes to a fantastic variety and number have been designed. Finally, many of these dressings made to represent the same type of natural fly, do not really closely resemble the original, and do not even resemble each other exactly. Is it necessary to have all these patterns or a large number of them?

It is not necessary. A really good angler might well wager that he could catch a trout with any one of them. The manner of presentation is more important than the fly. It is right to try to imitate a natural insect, but it is impossible to imitate them all, or to imitate any one absolutely exactly.

Observe the sketches I have made showing examples of the five main groups of flies with a breeding cycle which involves water. The drawings show the mature winged insect, but from the egg, each fly passes through several stages at each of which it has a different appearance. Most of them appear first as a tiny worm or grub. Some develop into a " creeper " form

D

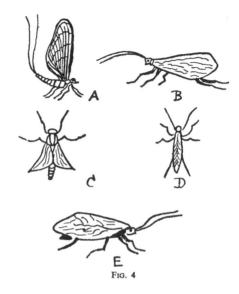

FIG. 4

TYPE OF INSECTS SHOWN ARE A—EPHEMERIDÆ, B—TRICHOP-
TERA, C—DIPTERA, D—PERLIDÆ AND E—SIALIDÆ

TABLE I

FLIES WITH LIFE-CYCLE INVOLVING WATER

The Ephemeridæ	Upright wings	This class includes all Duns and May flies.
The Trichoptera	Penthouse roof-shaped wings.	This class includes sedges.
The Perlidæ ..	Wings flat over body.	This class includes stone-flies, needles, willow-fly.
The Diptera ..	Two-winged flies.	This class includes gnats, cow-dung fly, daddy-long-legs.
The Sialidæ ..	Resembles Trichoptera.	Only one example—the alder.

NOTE.—The alder fly does not actually lay eggs in water
but on reeds, bushes and trees near water.

and most of them go through a pupa or chrysalis stage. On their way to the surface, just before changing into winged flies, they are described as " nymphs ". Artificial flies can be made to copy all of these forms, but a great many patterns have characteristics of shape, colour, apparent movement, any *one* of which may deceive trout and cause them to " have a go ". It has been shown that artificial flies in water *may cause vibrations or even sounds* which trout can detect and come to investigate.

Quite apart from the five groups mentioned there are tiny freshwater shrimps, fleas, snails and leeches, and of course, there are many insects which simply fall into the water. If the bottom of a small indoor aquarium were covered with samples of silt and debris taken from ponds and streams, a truly astonishing variety of " life " could be produced. Tiny creatures of all shapes, sizes and colours would move, flash and glint in the water. Hence the fly-dresser's use of tinsel, wire and bright " dubbings ".

Nowadays many anglers attempt to divide all flies into two classes—" imitators " and " attractors ". They have invented this second class " attractors " to cover all flies which they cannot identify as imitations of natural insects. The fault is theirs, and this distinction is as unsatisfactory as any other, for many so-called " attractors " *are* imitations, and *all* flies are intended to imitate " trout-food ".

I give below two short lists of dry flies and wet flies. I do not claim that they will cover every eventuality which an angler may encounter, but I am quite certain that any intelligent beginner will be successful and learn a lot by using them.

WET FLIES
Greenwell's Glory
Black Spider
Tup's Indispensable
Wickham's Fancy
Invicta
Alder
Woodcock and Mixed
Peter Ross
Kingfisher Butcher
Blue Zulu

DRY FLIES
Greenwell's Glory
Tup's Indispensable
Wickham's Fancy
Welshman's Button
Baigent's Brown
Red Quill
Iron Blue Dun
Willow Fly
Black Gnat
Cinnamon Sedge

Three flies appear in both lists. They are equally useful wet or dry. Many dry flies can be successfully used " wet ", and wet flies of the " hackle " type can be used " dry ".

The claim that flies-to-gut hang better than eyed-flies, cuts little ice nowadays, for eyed-flies are far more convenient in use.

CHAPTER V

SPINNING FOR TROUT

EVOLUTION AND PRESENT PRACTICE

THE earliest anglers used one rod for all purposes. Sometimes they used a minnow or " parr-tail " as bait and they cast it out in front of them and retrieved it by pulling the line through the rings by hand, or by moving the rod top. Later on they coiled the line on a tray strapped to their waists.

Since those days there has been a remarkable development in the equipment used. It began with the introduction of the Nottingham reel which was quickly improved by many patented devices. There followed the multiplier and the fixed-spool reel, and it is the last-named which holds the field to-day as the most efficient reel for the purpose.

It is possible to spin for trout using the earlier methods, but as the main task is to cast a very light bait far and control it accurately, using a light and inconspicuous line, all other reels must yield to the fixed-spool type with nylon line because this method achieves the angler's object superlatively well and no other method can approach it in efficiency to-day.

So efficient indeed, is the fixed-spool reel nowadays, that it has become something of a menace. There are times when it enables too many anglers to catch too many trout too often, and in a manner which is quite definitely inimical both to maintaining stocks of trout and to the use of the water for other kinds of fishing.

This unfortunate result is due to three main factors. Many waters contain trout of all ages and sizes. Very few anglers who use a fixed-spool reel in such places are able to use it discriminatingly—that is to say, in a way which will ensure that no small and immature fish are either " pricked," caught, damaged or scared. A minnow spun comparatively inexpertly and in the " easier " places, may yet have a fatal fascination for just those fish which it is desirable *not* to catch. A basket of trout with an average weight of half-a-pound caught in this way reflects little credit on the angler and provides poor sport. It usually means too that many smaller fish are damaged and scared and that the water is disturbed needlessly for other anglers.

Spinning for trout is banned on a great many fishings, not because it is an infallible means of taking fish (there are days when trout will not look at a minnow) but because of the harm it can do. Let us get this quite clear. There are baits which can be used legally, but which are not used for trout, and there are styles of rod-fishing which are legal but which are not tolerated for trout. Why? Simply because trout, pre-eminently among freshwater fish, can be caught in ways which are more satisfactory and pleasant.

With the prevalence of widespread abuse at the present day, a cautious and discriminating use of the fixed-spool reel for trout fishing has become one hall-mark of a good angler. The method is

not suitable for small and " nursery " streams.
It is unprofitable on fast-flowing and rocky
rivers, and it is out of place in the fly fishing
shallows of lakes and reservoirs.

THE PSYCHOLOGY OF SPINNING FOR TROUT

This criticism may seem both sweeping and
severe. Frankly, I am not sure that the main
trouble is not simply too many anglers and not
enough water. I was an adult fly fisher when I
bought my first fixed-spool reel. I did not like it.
I was not clever enough to use it skilfully and I
was too lazy to learn. Since then both reels and
lines have immensely improved. Any intelligent
child could learn to use them quickly and a great
many people begin angling with a spinning rod
and never use anything else. Fifty anglers on a
mile of river raking the water with fifty minnows
do not improve the fishing. Would fifty anglers
flogging the same water with one hundred and
fifty wet flies do less harm? It is a moot point,
and waters " flogged to death " were the cause of
complaint in the old days.

In my opinion the fifty wet fly anglers would
have more fun and more opportunity for skill, but
would I be of the same opinion if I had begun
fishing with a spinning reel and had never known
anything else? Nowadays a vicious circle is
completed. Too many fly fishers ruin a water:
spinning is then resorted to: sport rapidly de-
clines thereafter and neither method produces
fish while recrimination flourishes and blame is
freely allotted.

The late Alexander Wanless wrote many books about the use of the fixed-spool reel, and he devised many more or less complicated tackles under the firm conviction that *all* forms of fly and bait fishing could be better performed with these reels and light lines than in any other way. He believed that heavy lines and conventional fly and bait fishing would be as dead as the dodo in a few years following the introduction of his complete fixed-spool philosophy. That just did not happen. It may be too early yet to write with finality, but I am of the opinion that there is something basically satisfying about the casting of flies with conventional rods and heavy lines, and that particular physical delight will be given up no more readily than will all the rest of conventional fly fishing practice.

THE SPINNER'S TROUT

The legitimate quarry of the trout-spinner is the old and heavy fish which seldom rises to fly, which frequents places not easily accessible by other techniques, and which is wary of other baits but peculiarly susceptible to a spun minnow because small or injured fish offer the kind of bulky meal he needs to maintain his weight and condition.

Trout of this kind are found in lakes and ponds overgrown with weeds, in deep still reaches of rivers, in old flooded quarries and gravel-pits, and in the big lakes of all trout-countries. Such fish are great scavengers. They remind me of a rather silly conundrum. Why is it that a dog which eats flies never thrives? Because it never

gets enough of them! That seems to apply to
the big trout losing condition. The energy it
would have to expend in consuming sufficient
flies to do it any good, would make the business
unprofitable.

TROUT SPINNING TACKLE

The basis of the fixed-spool reel is a drum set
at right angles to the rod. Fine nylon line on
this drum is pulled off directly by the weight of
the bait when a cast is made. The line is re-
covered by a pick-up and " flier " which revolves
round the drum moved by gears when the handle
of the reel is turned.

I will not mention the name of the first reel of
this type which I owned in the early days. It
was not very satisfactory and I replaced it with a
Spinet which was a great improvement. Since
then I have had a number of reels, including
Altex, Ambidex and Mitchell. The latest reels
are beautifully made and most efficient. Automatic pick-up, slipping-clutch, and check with
adjustable tension are now almost standard
fittings, and usually two drums are supplied with
lines of different strengths. These are quickly
interchangeable.

Rods are five to nine feet long, but seven feet
is the most usual size. A certain amount of
" give " or butt-action is desirable, because the
cast is really a combination of swing and flick in
which the weight of the bait, however light,
should be felt. The main feature of modern rods
designed expressly for this kind of work, is the
placing of the few rings and graduation in size

from a very large and carefully placed butt-ring
to the tip. The object is to reduce friction and to
avoid kinking and tangles.

Lines are of nylon which may be either monofilament or braided. Braided line is supple
whereas monofilament tends to be too springy
but there is now such great competition between
makers of different brands, that the modern
product has been greatly improved and many
defects have been eradicated. In spinning for
trout, lines with a breaking strain of six pounds
should be regarded as the maximum. Two to
five pounds breaking strain nowadays means a
very fine line indeed.

It used to be considered wise to have the trace
of a weaker gauge so that, in the event of trouble
any breakage would occur there, and if the bait
were lost, the rest of the line would be saved.
I prefer to use an eighteen-inch long trace of fine
elasticum single-strand wire rather than nylon.
This has two swivels and a spring link for
attaching the bait. (Fig. 6).

The reel should be well filled to facilitate running off, but if it is too full, trouble will ensue.
The ideal is found by experiment.

Most anglers swear by natural baits and prefer
freshly caught dead minnows mounted on a tiny
Aerial tackle. Preserved minnows are said to be
less acceptable and artificial baits are scorned.
Great care is taken in the selecting and mounting
of dead minnows but most of this scrupulousness
is, in my opinion, misdirected. The early spinners
used a parr-tail, and experienced anglers know
well that there are easily-procured and legal baits
even more attractive than dead minnows. That

is to say, the idea that one is presenting a minnow
as if it were the exact imitation of a live minnow
is just nonsense. Whether the bait spins by
means of celluloid fins or wobbles due to the way
in which it is mounted, it does not greatly resemble
a live minnow and the fact is, that it need not do
so.

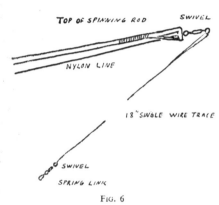

FIG. 6

SKETCH SHOWS EYE OF SWIVEL AGAINST ROD-TIP TO REDUCE
STRAIN ON LINE WHEN CASTING. SINGLE WIRE TRACE WITH
TWO SWIVELS AND SPRING LINK ATTACHMENT IS ALSO SHOWN

Devons, spoons, small plugs and some artificials can be used with good effect on occasion.
Two of these—imported production—baits are
still susceptible of improvement, and they are,
in my opinion, far too expensive. If the manufacturers have not the good sense to make them
in a better colour range and with finer wire and
more inconspicuous hooks and fittings, anglers

themselves will very soon be writing articles to
the angling Press describing how to make far
better baits of this kind at a fraction of the cost.

Years ago I urged British manufacturers to
make experiments in non-spinning artificials of
this kind, with particular regard to tiny jointed
plugs. Their productions in this field are still
either non-existent or ridiculously inadequate.

SPINNING TACTICS

The natural minnow is the most popular lure
and it is cast up, or up and across, in river and
stream fishing. Sometimes individual fish are
stalked, but the usual method is to search the
water systematically paying particular attention
to lies which are obviously likely to hold fish.
Overhead casts and side casts may be made as
circumstances dictate. Awkward places can be
reached by flicking the bait forward without any
swing backwards. When the bait enters the
water it is retrieved slowly and it should be
brought down with the current by winding the
reel handle at a speed which will keep it off the
bottom and simulate more or less the action of an
injured minnow.

Most of the usual cautions apply in spinning as
they do in other forms of angling. Keep out of
sight. Move slowly and wade only when
necessary and with the minimum of disturbance.

When fishing in lakes it pays to cast from rocky
promontories into deep water and to recover line
slowly towards the shallows. Such obvious lies
as the mouths of streams, submerged banks and
the lee of islands should be covered.

Continuous casting tends to weaken the last
few feet of line which should be examined and
cut off from time to time. Alternatively, this
strain can be minimized by winding up the line
until the trace swivel is hard against the rod top
and holding it there until the line is released in the
act of making the cast.

FIXED-SPOOL FRILLS

I have referred to the work of Alexander Wanless in developing spinning of this kind and in
elaborating uses of the fixed-spool reel. On the
Continent and in America the fixed-spool reel was
used with what has come to be known as a bubble-
float. This consisted of a hollow plastic ball of
transparent material with an " equitorial " flange
pierced for attachment to line and trace. It also
had a small " cap " which could be opened and
filled with water so as to give weight for casting
and yet retain enough air to give buoyancy so
that the " bubble " could act as a float. By
using this device it is possible to throw a long line
and yet have a visible mark which also suspends
either a cast of flies or a baited trace. This has
been used successfully in Britain both for fly and
bait fishing, but it is, in fact, a kind of float
fishing and is very much open to question as a
legitimate lure for trout and salmon.

Alexander Wanless wrote extensively to describe
elaborations of this principle. He made tiny
" air-floats " of quill or balsa wood and used the
weight and " mass " of these objects as a means of
casting a fine line from the fixed-spool reel.
Thrown before the wind, the air-floats remained

suspended in mid-air while from them descend
a cast of flies or a bait. The whole arrangeme
was a very delicate equipoise of fine tackle and
was claimed that, with skill, all the evolution
which fly fishers perform could be executed wi
a degree of precision and inconspicuous contr
which was impossible using heavy dressed lin
and conventional methods.

It will be obvious to anybody who uses a fixe
spool reel that many variations of other forms
angling are possible with it. But a float is a floa
whether it is in the air or the water, and whi
float-fishing is permissible for many forms
angling, it is not countenanced for the so-call
game fish. The fact is that devices of this kin
however delicately contrived and skilfully ope
ated, appear to approximate very closely in pri
ciple to certain engines which are definitely pr
hibited by law for the taking of salmon and trou
The otter, cross-lines and trimmers are very cru
and effective ways of destroying fish. Air-floa
no less than bubble-floats are not very far m
moved from such engines in principle. If the
ever became widely used it is not unlikely th
some strange border-line cases would come befo
the courts, for the kind of people who are no
prosecuted for offences of this type, would eager
set themselves to the task of bringing the tw
methods—the use of floats and the use of illeg
engines—even more closely together than th
are at present. This is, of course, a personal a
purely speculative opinion. The development
light-line-and-controller methods of fishing ma
proceed to oust older methods as their chi
protagonist foretold. Alexander Wanless did

great deal to advance fixed-spool reel technique, and if he had not written on the side of skill and delicacy, the use of the reel might have been attended with far greater abuses than it has been. These methods of fishing with bubble-floats and controllers exist, and they have been extensively described. I also describe them here. Any angler who wishes is free to experiment with them, but he should be warned that normal fixed-spool spinning is subject to abuse and that these other methods may have even greater potentialities in that direction.

CHAPTER VI

RODS

TROUT rods are made of greenheart, split-cane,
glass fibre or steel. They act as a means of pro-
jecting a line ending in a hook into the " path "
of a fish, and they also act as a " spring " to keep
the line taut once a fish is hooked, and to absorb
to some extent the tension which a hooked fish
places on fine tackle.

The strength of a rod is not judged by the weight
which it can lift; it is judged by the stiffness of its
" action ". No trout rod need ever be able to
lift a weight of one pound into the air, but a good
trout rod weighing six ounces can be used to play
and land a fish weighing twenty pounds.

The only worth while advice which it is possible
to give in a book on the subject of buying rods is,
take an experienced angler to advise on the pur-
chase, and be sure that you examine the rod
assembled, and fitted with a reel and line of the
proper weight.

I give below a rough and ready table showing
the lengths and " actions " of rods used for trout
fishing. Rods longer than ten feet or heavier
than twelve ounces are out of place in trout
fishing. A stiffish action is to be recommended
for dry fly work and a less stiff action for
everything else.

TABLE II

TROUT RODS

MATERIAL: Split-Cane, Greenheart, Glass-Fibre or Steel

Purpose	Length	Action	Reel	Line
Dry Fly	7–10 feet	Stiff	Fly	Tapered: Dressed Silk.
Wet Fly	9–11 feet	Butt-action	Fly	Level: Dressed Silk.
Upstream Bait	9–11 feet	Butt-action	Fly or Fixed-Spool	Level; Dressed Silk (or nylon).
Dapping	15 feet	Stiff	Wood or Plastic	Floss Silk or Cotton.
Spinning	6–9 feet	Butt-action	Fixed-Spool	Nylon: braided or monofilament.

REELS

Reels should be made of light non-corrosive alloy. They should have narrow drums and line-guard and be free of gadgets.

LINES

Lines used in fly and bait fishing are comparatively heavy and they are dressed either with oil or with some other preparation to render them at once smooth and supple yet stiff. This is the point which beginners do not realize. Limp lines are useless for fly fishing. A line of dressed silk may be either " level " (the same thickness throughout its length) or single-tapered or double-tapered. Tapering assists in casting.

Spinning lines may be of silk or braided cotton,

E

but nylon and other synthetics, either monofilament or braided, are now most commonly
used and are highly satisfactory. Spinning lines
are fine, light and limp.

LEADERS AND TRACES

Leaders are sometimes referred to as " casts ",
but as the word has other meanings in angling,
" leader " is to be preferred. This is a length of
fine transparent material used between line and
hook. Horsehair used to be used for the purpose until it was superseded by gut. Now
nylon, which is much cheaper than gut, is most
commonly used. In spinning, the place of the
leader is taken by the " trace ", although the
word leader is also used. Traces can be either
of gut or nylon or fine single-strand wire, or of
several fine strands twisted together.

GENERAL

The complete assembly of rod, reel, line,
leader and hook, ought to match with the object
of deceiving the fish by a blend of inconspicuous-
ness and skilful manipulation by remote control
of the hook. For this reason many modern
anglers insist that the rod exactly suitable for one
particular job should be used. Thus, a long stiff
rod is most suitable for upstream worming, a
short stiff rod for dry fly work, a long butt-
actioned rod for big rivers and loch fishing with
wet fly, and so on. All that is a trifle unrealistic
because conditions vary so much. The theory
that a set of many matched golf clubs is of great

assistance to the golfer is based on half-a-dozen blatant fallacies—that all men are expert judges of distance, that golf courses are of a uniform and billiard table smoothness, that wind, weather, temperament and physique are constant, etc. Old time golfers with cleek, mashie and putter, could make nonsense of this theory, and in the same way a nine-foot trout rod in skilful hands may be adapted to many uses and occasions. The trout fisher who gets most fun out of his fishing is the " all-rounder " rather than the specialist.

Over the years fishermen collect favourite rods for special occasions. Most of them do so, but it is better to be able to use one good rod really well than to be an indifferent performer with half a dozen. Only as a result of practical experience with one rod, can an angler judge its efficiency and shortcomings in enabling him to do what he requires it to do. When he finds out its limitations he is far better able to judge what improvements and modifications are necessary in a rod designed expressly for some special purpose. Experience of this kind is a pleasure to acquire. A three-piece ten-foot rod of rather stiff action has an all round usefulness. Such a rod is light and easy to carry. It is also convenient for travel and storing, and it will serve for upstream worming and for wet and dry fly work on rivers and lakes. A rod of this kind is an excellent " first " rod. As the basis of any collection it gives the angler not only a sound appreciation of what it can do, but also, as his experience grows, a good indication of what it cannot do and what it should not be expected to do.

LEADERS, KNOTS AND HOOKS

Nylon is now so reliable, so uniform, and so cheap, that it is tending to supplant gut for

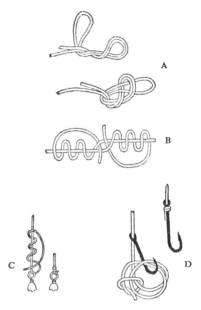

Fig. 7

KNOTS FOR NYLON. TO MAKE A LOOP, USE "A" DOUBLE OVERHAND LOOP. TO JOIN TWO LENGTHS OF NYLON (OR USE END FOR DROPPER) USE "B" THE BLOOD KNOT. TO ATTACH LINE TO SWIVEL EYE, USE "C." FOR ATTACHING NYLON TO EYED HOOK, USE "D," THE DOUBLE TURLE KNOT

leaders and traces. Because it is so smooth and hard, it is inclined to cut through itself under strain when tied in the old conventional fishermen's knots which were used for gut. New knots expressly designed for nylon have been invented. Those which are illustrated opposite are simple enough and should be learnt. It is a good plan to buy several spools of nylon of various gauges and breaking-strain. By making up one's own leaders, " tapers " can be devised to suit special requirements.

Use only the best eyed hooks for trout fishing. The eyed type of hook is convenient, and the best should be insisted upon if only to avoid that most disappointing of all trout-fishers' tales—the one about the unexpectedly heavy fish which " straightened out the hook."

MISCELLANEOUS

Cigarette tins of the kind known as " flat-fifties " are most useful as containers for trout-tackle. They serve as holders for made-up leaders, as fly-boxes (when fitted with strips of felt) and as receptacles for traces, leads and minnows. Plastic mounts are now available for leaders. These are very handy and save time, but if dealers would only sell them at one third of their present price they would sell twenty times more than they do at present. Until they learn sense, their customers will do well to use four-inch squares of thin cardboard cut as shown in the adjoining sketch. (Fig. 8).

Trout fishers travel light. This takes a good deal of shrewd organizing and contriving. It means that such things as landing-nets, creels, fishing-bags and clothing are chosen deliberately for reasons of convenience and lightness and

general suitability for the job. Knives, scissors
and bottle-openers demand safe and accessible
pockets. There should be a place for all neces-

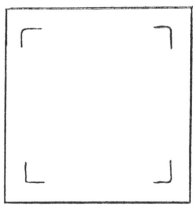

FIG. 8
THIN SQUARE CARD, ABOUT 4 IN. BY 4 IN. TO WIND
LEADER ON

sities without over-elaboration so that a quick
check-up can be made at any time to see that
everything is present and correct.

CHAPTER VII

CASTING

GENERAL

I USED to think that any intelligent person who was reasonably athletic and possessed a good eye could learn to cast in a matter of minutes. For that reason I had little time for descriptions in books aided by either diagrams or photographs. I find that I am wrong. A friend of mine who can do most other things reasonably well is quite unable to cast. There is some defect in his imagination or co-ordination of hand and eye which prevents him succeeding.

For all that I still do not believe that much can be learnt either from written description or pictures. In casting, the " feel " of the process is everything and should be at once completely explanatory and revealing. I was surprised to read recently of a casting instructor whose pupil suddenly exclaimed, " I get it now! It's exactly like flicking balls of clay off the end of a twig! " This most curious and unexpected simile was exactly paralleled by a Canadian who informed me that he only understood what I was demonstrating when he recalled how he and his brother as kids used to have battles in an apple orchard by sticking canes in windfalls and flicking them at each other.

The point of these tales is that casting is a misleading sight to the unthinking observer. He thinks that it is the movement of the rod which causes the projection of the line, and fails to realize that it is the *checking* of the movement which is the really important part of the process. The other secret in learning to cast, is to learn to pause long enough for the line to extend behind before starting any forward movement.

CASTING A FLY

The rod moves quickly in a comparatively small arc—say thirty degrees, and it is checked, more or less violently, at both the limits of this arc. The check causes the line to extend behind, and then to the front, *after which the rod is moved slowly forward.*

Practice on the lawn. Use a short line to start. Lengthen it later. Do not hesitate to *look behind* you in practice in order to see the speed at which the line is extending. Once you can cast overhand with the right hand, try sideways casting at waist level. Then try casting " backhand " over the left shoulder, and afterwards try all of these movements using the left hand.

CASTING A SPINNING BAIT

Using a fixed-spool reel, press the line against the rod between reel and butt-ring with the forefinger while swinging the bait as it hangs from the rod-point. This gives the " feel " of the cast. *Without any violence* swing the bait from rear to front and release the line by removing forefinger. The exact moment for release, and the precise degree of force will be learnt by practice. Side-casts and variations should be tried just as in fly-casting.

In both bait and fly casting practice, the object should be to attain ease and accuracy before worrying about distance. There is no great virtue in being able to cast far without accuracy.

FORM

I recently listened to two young men discussing " form " in rowing. My memory went back thirty years to similar discussions, and then I thought of many shrewd comments made when a Russian crew scored a brilliant success at Henley this year. Is there not some truth in the criticism that the decline in British supremacy in sport and games may be due to an altogether misguided and ridiculous osbsesion with " form " ? For fifty years British rowing men have been arguing their heads off about the best way to tie themselves in knots in boats. Along comes a crew of Russians single-mindedly concerned with winning. Like General Sherman in war, they believed that winning meant simply " to git thar fustest with the mostest men ".

The human body and mind and temperament has infinite variation in the individual. There is no one method and style for playing cricket or golf or riding a horse into which everybody must be crammed holus-bolus to secure the best results. But there is an *optimum* result which every individual can attain by adapting certain basic principles to his own requirements.

I am writing this as introductory comment before explaining my attitude to the position

which "casting" holds in the sport of fishing.
Anglers often invite me to agree with them in
saying that the ability to exercise the maximum
variety in method, and maximum degree of
accuracy and distance with any given equipment,
has not a great deal to do with good fishing into
which so many other considerations must enter.
I am inclined to disagree. I attach great im-
portance to "presentation", and the casting of
a fly or bait the "presenting" of it on the water
in the right place and manner, cannot be rele-
gated to any minor position in the scale of things.
A sportsman who takes only the dead-easy birds
while out shooting learns little, and makes slow
progress. The angler who tries only for "sitters"
in the way of easy fish will miss a lot of fun.
It is the difficult fish which provide the best sport,
and to reach them one *must* be able to cast with
some versatility and skill. How is this ability to
be acquired?

The beginning angler should seek opportunities of handling as many outfits as possible.
He will be surprised at the variety he will encounter. There will be stiff rods, slack rods,
"dead" rods, lively rods, tip-actioned rods, and
butt-actioned rods. Many of them will be fitted
with lines which are too light, and a few of them
will have lines which are too heavy. After a while
he will begin to see where his own outfit fits in to
the scheme of things. Some of the other rods
will not suit him so well as his own, and others of
them will act better than his.

In exactly the same way, by watching other
people casting, he will find some worse than
himself and others better.

Once he has acquired the experience to know the combination of rod and line most suited to his own requirements, he can keep a look out for the ideal outfit. He should also avoid the errors of people who cast worse than he does, and copy the methods of his betters. There are very few anglers in this country to-day who would not benefit from the assistance which a good casting instructor can give. Those who are not too frightened to discover how " bad " they are, should enter for amateur events in a casting tournament, or they should engage in some practical comparisons of their ability with their friends. Nobody need be at all abashed or down-cast to find that he has a lot to learn. With the right outfit, casting is one of the easiest things to learn, and it is an activity in which remarkable progress can be made in a very short time.

It is not, however, an end in itself, and practice should always have some relation to the kind of experience or problem which is likely to be encountered in practical angling. There is one exception to that statement. The present high average standard of performance of modern rods is due to the experiments made by professional casters with special equipment supplied to them by manufacturers. Anybody who finds that he has a flair for casting and a desire to exploit it in this way should carry on with the good work, and good luck to him!

The advice at the beginning of this chapter is confined to nothing more than two or three " tips " because I believe that diagrams and written descriptions can do a beginner more harm than good. The observations about

" form " and the position of casting in the sport
of angling are based on another conviction. To
advise anybody to keep a straight bat while
playing cricket, or to adopt a forward seat while
riding without actually seeing the bat and the
seat and the dimensions of the owner, is a waste of
time.

CHAPTER VIII

TROUT WATERS

STREAMS, BROOKS, BURNS AND BECKS

THESE are the waters of the moors and uplands. The fishing they provide is excellent practice for other kinds of angling, and it is particularly suitable for the beginner for a number of reasons. Firstly, the terrain compels the right kind of approach, and in the second place, results are nearly always forthcoming.

This does not mean that small waters are necessarily easy, or that they are only fit for beginners. Fishing in moorland streams is a delightful and solitary pursuit which lures the angler into picturesque country and also offers the expert plenty of scope for his virtuosity in skilfully fishing those " lies " likely to produce the heaviest fish. Wet fly is likely to be most productive, but the dry fly is by no means excluded and upstream worming is also profitable.

DEEP SLOW RIVERS

The clear water of spring-fed chalk streams in southern England is the classic home of the dry-fly. This is the method most suited to smooth weedy reaches haunted by really heavy fish which rise freely to the floating fly. At the same time there are rivers all over Britain which at times produce hatches of fly and have slow deep reaches

77

providing sport equal to that of the famous Hampshire rivers. The dry fly can be used to fish the rise wherever it is evident, and a single nymph or team of three wet flies can be used in the absence of visible rises.

A judicious use of the fixed-spool reel may be justified in cases where old bottom-feeding trout are present in selected " holts." Such fish are better out of this kind of water and spinning is often the best means of removing them.

FAST AND ROCKY RIVERS

This category includes the headwaters of the great salmon rivers as well as shorter streams of the more impetuous kind. Dry fly and light spinning are seldom satisfactory here. Fast flowing broken water makes it difficult to avoid " drag "—that bugbear of the dry fly angler, and light lines come to grief where snags are the rule rather than the exception.

This kind of river often holds good trout and the conventional wet fly fisher is given full opportunity to use his skill and knowledge. Alternatively, the upstream worm in clear water will produce results.

LAKES, LOCHS, AND LOUGHS

Here lies the greatest hope for the waterless angler. So much stress has been laid on the joy of river-fishing in the past, that these immense fisheries have been, comparatively speaking, neglected. As a rule it is both cheaper and easier to obtain permission to fish in lakes, and the great

British lakes offer scope for every kind of trout-
fishing. Spinning, trailing, dapping, wet and dry
fly can all be practised at the right time and place.
Where is the right place and what is the right
time? These are matters to be discovered by
intelligent reconnaissance. Lake fishers should
be glad that enterprise and intelligence are so
necessary in their craft, for these requirements
thin out " the field " considerably in the race for
good fishing.

RESERVOIRS

There are already many reservoirs in Britain
and there are going to be a great many more.
Fishing is allowed in some of them and it ought
to be permitted in all of them. There are certain
advantages about fishing in these waters. The
fishing is usually supervised and free from
pollution and predators. As a rule spinning is
barred.

Trout in reservoirs are sometimes said to
acquire the reservoir habit of feeding on the
surface only at dawn and dusk. This is seldom a
just criticism, but even if it were, there are legitimate methods of catching reservoir trout on
fly even in the absence of surface-feeding fish.
Space does not allow of a detailed description of
such methods here, but the angler who intends
to do much reservoir-fishing cannot do better
than refer to a book entitled *Still Water Fly
Fishing* by T. C. Ivens.

CHAPTER IX

THE RIVER TYRANTS

IT has already been explained that the size of trout is directly related to feeding. There comes a time in the life of a strong healthy trout when it must feed either very much faster or adopt a more bulky diet in order to maintain its weight. Insect food appears to be necessary to all trout. The fat content of insects is greater than the fat content of minnows and small freshwater fish, but in order to keep in good condition, heavy trout must sooner or later supplement their normal diet with small fish.

The small fish which big trout eat are only small in a comparative sense. " I have seen large Thames trout," wrote Francis Francis in 1865, " of eight, ten and twelve pounds weight chasing roach of half and three-quarters of a pound, and even larger ones, scores of times; and I have always found, on examining trout that have been caught, when they have had fish in them, that the fish they had chosen to devour were good-sized ones, much larger indeed than the Thames anglers usually employ as a bait."

Such fish are more destructive than pike. They do a great deal of harm and they should be fair game to any angler able to locate them and to work out a plan for their capture. Big trout are tough customers, and they have grown big because their reflexes are quick and conditioned through

long experience to react to danger or any sus-
picious circumstances. Big trout are extremely
wary as a rule. That is why they have grown big.

To catch trout of this kind calls for a campaign
and a close study of the fish's individual habits.
Spinning, bobbing the minnow, or dapping at
dusk with an enormous hackled fly are methods
most likely to succeed. The principle of big bait
for a big fish seems to be clearly established for
the really " outsize " trout.

SALMO FEROX

In the past I have been criticized for using the
name *Salmo ferox*. " These are simply great lake
trout ", wrote one scribe by way of correction.
The term ferox is used not to imply that huge
trout of this type are a separate species, but
simply for convenience. To call them " great
lake trout " is misleading on two counts. The
great lake trout of America is really a char.
The British ferox is found, not in lakes but in the
deep waters of Scotland and Ireland, where there
are very few " lakes ". The name ferox is much
more correct and apt to indicate what I mean,
and I propose to continue to use it.

Francis wrote:

" Common trout in lakes often increase to a
large size; but there is a trout peculiar to lakes,
called the great lake-trout, or salmo-ferox.
When full grown, the ferox is a handsome fish
in appearance, but his flesh is coarse, and as an
adjunct to the table, he is not in very great
esteem. As a matter of sport, he is one of the
strongest and gamest fish that swims when you

F

have hooked him; and the killing of a 20 lb.
ferox is no light triumph and no easy achieve-
ment—a 30 lb. salmon is a much easier con-
quest. But they rarely take anything but a
trolling bait, and that at long and weary intervals, seldom indeed rising to a fly (though
have known them taken with it)."

In order to arrive at some conclusions which
form a basis for a modern approach to the
catching of ferox, it is of interest to study what
has already been written on the subject. Let us
see what the late P. D. Malloch had to say about
ferox.

"Its great size is accounted for by the fact
that it has become a cannibal and lives almost
entirely on its own species. I have made a
point of examining most of those I got in
nearly all of which contained from one to three
trout and nothing else. Where there are plenty
of trout to feed upon, they grow so quickly that
they may be 15 to 20 lbs. in weight in seven or
eight years. For their size they weigh much
more than salmon and far surpass them in
strength. When hooked they fight to the last
often escaping when they are in the net or on
the gaff. They are usually caught by trolling
with artificial minnow, but the most successful
bait is a small trout. It is best to have one rod
mounted with a phantom and another with a
small trout trolled between the deep and the
shallow water. I have found that they take
best on a dull and fairly rough day. They are
now so much sought after however, that a good
deal of patience is required to catch one, and
blank days are the rule."

Writing in 1888, Charles St. John discussed ferox at some length and gave interesting directions about trolling for them.

"The only way to kill the larger trout is by trolling. In Loch Awe and several other lochs I have seen this kind of fishing succeed well. If the sportsman is skilful, he is sure of taking finer trout in this way than he would ever do when fly fishing. In trolling there are two or three rules which should be carefully observed:—

"Choose the roughest wind that your boat can live in; fish with a good-sized bait, not much less than a herring, and do not commence your trolling till after two o'clock in the afternoon, by which time the large fish seem to have digested their last night's supper and to be again on the move. You may pass over the heads of hundreds of large trout when they are lying at rest and not hungry, and you will not catch one; but as soon as they begin to feed, a fish, although he may have half a dozen small trout in his stomach, will still run at your bait. The weight of sinkers on your line, and the depth at which you fish, must of course depend on the depth of water in the loch. A patient fisherman should find out how deep every reach and bay is before he begins to troll. The labour of a day spent in taking soundings is well repaid. The strength and activity of the large loch trout is immense, and he will run out your whole reel-line if allowed to do so. Sometimes he will go down perpendicularly to the bottom, where he remains sulky or attempts to rub off the hooks: get him out of this situation and away he goes, almost towing your boat after him. Then is the time for your boatman to make play to keep up with the fish and save your line, for a twenty-pound salmo ferox is no ignoble foe to contend with when you have him at the end of a common fishing-line: he appears to have the strength of a whale as he rushes away."

FEROX TACKLE AND TACTICS

All of these writers stress the decline in quantity and weight of ferox, and Malloch, Francis and many others bewail the wearisomeness of un-rewarded trolling. St. John advocates no earlier start than afternoon, and quite a number of authorities recommend trolling in the dark. It seems clear that towards the end of last century trolling for ferox was a popular sport and that many lochs were denuded of heavy fish in consequence. What is the position to-day?

Such lochs as Awe, Rannoch, Ericht, Ness, Laggan, Tay, Shin and Urigill (to mention only a few) still contain heavy trout with this special deep-water cannibalistic way of life, but the average weight seems to have declined. The advice to fish in the hours of darkness is sound. Fish feed near the surface in darkness because certain minute organisms on which they feed are only to be found near the surface after dark. It would be reasonable to expect fish which prey on the smaller fish to follow them up from the depths.

Trolling for ferox needs a long stiff rod. I use a converted greenheart salmon rod. The butt and mid-section have been fitted with special porcelain rings. A large wooden reel is used. A Crocodile mount is good, but the best is probably Malloch's Butcher tackle designed specifically for the job. This mount allows of a half-pound trout being used with a wobbling movement. A wire trace with half-a-pound of lead is not too much to get the bait down.

Trolling for ferox with this kind of tackle is an uncertain business. Even with an intimate know-ledge of the underwater contours and considerable persistence in trolling slowly into the wind, it seems plain that although many fish are " covered" they may refuse to co-operate. It may well be as St. John suggests that the fish are gorged with the previous night's repast. At all events they take better in darkness.

With the rod described I have tried spinning with a Silex reel and a half-pound trout as bait! That is a somewhat strenuous proceeding and better results are achieved with a multiplier and a short rod. Alone after midnight in the middle of Loch Shin I once hooked a ferox on a five-foot steel rod with offset handle and Elarex reel using nine pound b.s. Nyking. The bait was a half-pound trout on Butcher tackle and I had been laboriously lobbing this burden into the darkness and listening for the splash before counting " twenty " and beginning to wind slowly in. The bait was taken with such violence that I was nearly pulled overboard. Half an hour later I managed to get the fish alongside and then pro-ceeded to knock it off the hooks while attempting to gaff it. The moral of this story is, always have a companion to manage the boat when playing a ferox in the dark.

Very few sports can compare with trout fishing in the matter of variety of method and scene. The hill-loch, the moorland stream, and the lowland river offer chances of recreation which can be idyllic, but for the angler who wants an occasional touch of adventure coupled with a sense of grappling with the unknown, spinning for ferox in the deep Scottish and Irish waters offers great opportunities. There is a vogue nowadays for big-fish hunting regarded as a special problem for individual solution. The ferox is the trout-fisher's equivalent of the specimen carp and the giant pike, which need special study.

CHAPTER X

IN CONCLUSION

SOME NOTABLE TROUT

THE number of duly authenticated British trout which have been caught weighing over ten pounds must run into hundreds if not thousands, and there must be a great many fish of this size which have never been weighed or recorded. No useful purpose is served by attempting to give a complete list, or even a list of recent captures. There are, however, some almost legendary trout whose capture has been attended by unusual circumstances, and there are some fish caught in recent years which show that really big trout are still catchable and that the type is widely dispersed. A selection of such fish is noted below.

Weight	Place	Year	Captor
*39½ lb. ..	Loch Awe ..	1866	William Muir
†29 lb. ..	Loch Stennes	1899	—
27½ lb. ..	River Tay ..	1842	Col. Dobiggin
21 lb. ..	Loch Rannoch	1904	Miss Kate Kirby
20 lb. ..	Loch Corrib ..	1925	T. Harris
18¾ lb. ..	Loch Mask ..	1934	T. Malley
18 lb. ..	New River, Hornsey.	1907	J. Briggs
18 lb. ..	River Test, Broadlands.	1922	Brig.-Gen. T. Hickman
16 lb. 15 oz.	River Thames	1880	Mr. Wicks
16¼ lb. ..	Loch Corrib ..	1936	A. L. Spiers
14 lb. ..	Loch Rannoch	1932	A. S. Roe
13 lb. 3 oz.	River Lee, Hertford.	1907	—

*This is the famous British record trout caught by William Muir of Innistrynich. It was foul-hooked when he was fishing for salmon. It took two hours to land.

†Loch Stennes water is " brackish " after high tides. The fish was caught on a hand-line.

NOTABLE TROUT OF THE FUTURE

What is the prospect facing the modern seeker of big trout? For many years writers have deplored diminishing stocks of fish, and a decrease in average size. In the good old days when enormous baskets were recorded, the bulk of the catch consisted of small fish but there were far more big fish also caught then, than there are nowadays. I am inclined to be optimistic and to think that the phase of small trout and rare " specimens " is drawing to a close.

The fame of Blagdon reservoir has had a good effect. The remarkably fine trout which it has produced have stimulated other fishery authorities to investigate the possibilities of emulating Blagdon. The knowledge and experience which the Blagdon people have acquired will no doubt bear fruit, not only in new reservoirs near Bristol, but also much farther afield.

Local authorities have certain advantages in preserving the fishing in reservoirs of this kind. They have complete control. The three pernicious P's, poaching, pollution and predators, are kept in check, and it is possible to control the stock of fish with the object of maintaining a high average weight. As there are a great many new reservoirs in course of construction, and an increasing number of anglers, there is some likelihood of local authorities striving to combine efficient town-supply of water with really good trout fishing.

In Scotland and Wales the depredations of hydro-electric authorities may be largely offset by similar endeavours. The great advantage of having complete control of an entire catchment area cannot be denied. Already some visionaries are citing the enormous increase in angling resources which has resulted in America in the Tennessee Valley, as a result of a large new area being under a single authority. They say that half-a-dozen schemes on a much smaller scale in this country will provide better angling for much larger numbers than formerly.

There is another aspect of such activities. A good deal of research is being conducted into the conditions which make for trout growth and healthy stocks of fish. Some experiments have been made in the fertilization of waters with a view to increasing plankton, and, in that way, the size of the fish. Although it is too early yet to anticipate the practical application of these methods deliberately carried out, the fact remains that trout in certain districts are already showing an increased average weight, purely as a result of the leaching of agricultural fertilizers into waters during and since the last war.

In pre-war days the large bottom-feeding trout was rather a problem. Anglers used to say that he was " better out of the water ", but in large lakes and river-systems the phrase was little more than a pious hope. Nowadays the position is somewhat changed. Firstly, there is the vogue (which I have already mentioned) of big-fish-hunting. People make a deliberate study of the conditions of life among these bottom-feeding trout, and they make special plans to angle for them. Secondly, there have been great advances made in fine spinning tackle using nylon lines on reels which are a great improvement on the earlier models. Finally, there are complete ranges of new synthetic materials being used, not

only for fly-dressing, but for the devising of lures
and spinners with novel " actions " and in some
cases luminous and daylight-fluorescent qualities.
The large bottom-feeding trout of the big lakes
and great rivers is now far more vulnerable than
formerly.

TROUT COOKERY

In days gone by there was a pleasant custom
of presenting the catch or part of the catch to one's
host, or to the boatman or ghillie or other assist-
ant, and if the catch were a remarkably fine one,
the fish could be sent to the nearest hospital. This
practice has sadly declined. It should be restored.

Some anglers make gifts of trout to their
friends, but quite often this practice merely em-
barrasses a career-girl wife, so great has been the
decline in the domestic virtues. It seems to be a
matter for regret that our national mania for fried
fish (fried by somebody else) should result in
nearly every fish being fried on sight. I do not
exaggerate. In that admirable monthly, *Angling*,
there appeared recently an article written by a
lady who began by informing her readers that
she was noted for her fine recipes for cooking
trout. She then proceeded to give half-a-dozen
examples. They all involved frying!

The trout is an eminently edible fish and lends
itself admirably to the practice of culinary ex-
pertise. It should be the duty of every trout
fisher who does not return fish to the water alive, to
make sure that his catch is treated with care and
respect. If he can find nobody capable of cooking
it properly he should learn to do the job himself.

Trout up to two or three pounds may be

cooked by boiling, baking, stewing or grilling.
Small fish are excellent eating and a fish of two
pounds, if in good condition and having pink
flesh, can be carefully boiled and served cold
with salad.   The flesh of heavier trout is inclined
to be coarse and requires special attention.

The angler determined to cook his own fish
should don soft-soled shoes and creep to the
kitchen and lock himself in.   He should then
produce from an inside pocket his own special
case of really-sharp knives, and set to work.   If
he understands the use of such aids as white wine,
bay leaves and chervil, so much the better, if not,
why not experiment and learn?

Boiled trout: Gut and dry the fish.   Place in a
deep pan of boiling water.   Throw in a small
quantity of salt and some vinegar.   Boil gently
for twenty minutes.   Serve on crisp toast with
melted butter, chopped parsley and pepper.

Stewed trout: Ingredients: Two medium-sized
trout, half sliced onion, a little parsley, one bay
leaf and a blade of mace, salt and pepper, one
pint medium stock.

Wash the fish clean and wipe dry.   Lay in
stewpan with all ingredients.   Simmer for half-
an-hour.   Take out, strain gravy and add thicken-
ing, and stir these over a sharp fire for five
minutes, then pour over fish and serve.

Grilled trout: Make a few sharp incisions on
the flanks of each fish.   Smear with olive oil and
sprinkle with salt and pepper.   Grill carefully
and gently for five to ten minutes, turning the fish
several times and then serve with a sauce to suit.

Baked trout: Gut and dry the fish.   Squeeze
the juice of a lemon over it, then salt, pepper,

chopped parsley and chopped chives. Lay on well-buttered dish and bake in oven for ten minutes. Serve with suitable sauce.

Although I have put " boil ", fish should never be briskly boiled but rather " poached ": that is to say, as soon as the liquid appears to be on the point of boiling, the cooking vessel should be placed on a place where it will be hot enough to keep it in that almost-boiling state for some time.

Fish should be fresh clean and dry. It is a first-class mistake to gut fish unnecessarily at the waterside and to stuff them with grass, or wrap them in leaves or rushes with a view to preserving them during transport. Dampness and heat are the causes of decomposition as often as not, and attempts to clean and wrap the fish usually defeat the object for which they are practised.

If kept clean and dry (a little salt *may* help here) trout will keep for not more than thirty-six hours in cool and unexposed conditions. If sent by post or rail, the fish should be sewn in a reed " bass " and plainly labelled with the time of capture, and the consignee should be invariably advised by phone or wire in order to avoid disappointment and sad accidents.

TROUT FISHER'S PHILOSOPHY

To suggest that angling is no more than " escapism " is to put the sport on a par with the cinema, television and football pools. That is quite obviously ridiculous. The enduring and increasing popularity of angling springs from its ability to draw men back into the open air and to the countryside with a keen appreciation of nature and a proper delight in the fact that they fit into the picture and can engage in activities involving manual dexterity and mental agility *for their own sake.*

Although trout fishing is a solitary and contemplative pastime, like-minded men take pleasure in meeting each other, and there is an extensive lore and literature which all fishermen share.

If in this book I have appeared to show prejudice in praising or decrying some kinds of angling, I have done so because I believe that self-discipline and self-rule are characteristic angling virtues. In such games as golf, cricket and rugby football, and in sports like field athletics, sportsmanship (which is self-discipline) is being ousted by a mass of rule and regulation which should be unnecessary and is harmful. The sea-lawyers, the accountants, and the professionals are making sport a business and destroying its essence. We do not want angling to be ruled and regulated so that initiative is restricted. Unwritten rules are best for anglers and only experience will show their wisdom.

Nevertheless all trout fishers have certain responsibilities. They are able to fish for trout because in the past other people have been to some trouble to foster the sport and to protect and preserve trout fisheries. The present day angler has an obligation to continue this good work. The best way to do this is by example rather than precept, for there is perhaps a deal too much " nattering " about everything nowadays and not enough action. To show that I am sometimes capable of practising what I preach, I bring this little book to a close and announce my intention of going fishing forthwith. Tight lines!

INDEX

95